DEADLY
DISASTERS

TRUE HAUNTINGS

DEADLY DISASTERS

DINAH WILLIAMS

SCHOLASTIC PRESS / NEW YORK

Copyright © 2020 by Dinah Dunn

All rights reserved. Published by Scholastic Press, an imprint of Scholastic Inc., *Publishers since 1920*. SCHOLASTIC, SCHOLASTIC PRESS, and associated logos are trademarks and/or registered trademarks of Scholastic Inc.

Library of Congress Cataloging-in-Publication Data

Names: Williams, Dinah (Dinah J.), author.
Title: True hauntings : deadly disasters / Dinah Williams.
Description: First edition. | New York : Scholastic Press, 2020.
Identifiers: LCCN 2019006594 | ISBN 9781338355840 (pbk. : alk. paper)
Subjects: LCSH: Ghosts—Juvenile literature. | Natural disasters—Miscellanea—Juvenile literature.
Classification: LCC BF1473 .W55 2020 | DDC 133.1—dc23

10 9 8 7 6 5 4 3 2 1   20 21 22 23 24

Printed in the U.S.A.   40

First edition, June 2020

Book design by Kay Petronio

To my terrific parents,
whose unconditional support
has made me brave

CONTENTS

INTRODUCTION

*Spookiness is the real purpose of the ghost
story. It should give you the creeps
and disturb your thoughts . . .*

—Roald Dahl

Throughout human history, people have believed in
ghosts, which are thought to be human spirits that continue to exist after the body has died. One of the earliest
recorded ghost sightings was in Rome in the first century
AD, at a local bathhouse that was haunted by the angry
spirit of a man murdered there.

And many people still do believe. In a recent survey,
nearly 20 percent were convinced that they have seen or
been in the presence of a ghost. One out of every five people! If you've picked up this book about true hauntings,
you probably believe in ghosts as well. Maybe you've even
seen one yourself.

But why do ghosts appear? According to psychic
research, earthbound spirits are often caused when

someone dies unexpectedly. Their death comes as a shock, so they may not know or accept that they are dead. They become stuck either where they died or where they spent their lives. Their presence can be seen, felt, heard—or even smelled! Maybe they make themselves known with footsteps down an empty hall or an odd cold spot in a warm room. Oftentimes ghosts are seen on an anniversary of a tragic event, because that's when the memory is strongest.

Ghost hunters have tried to gather evidence of their existence, such as images of spirits in photographs and sounds on audiotape. But the only solid proof we have that ghosts exist is what people have seen or felt in a particular place. That is the basis for many of the stories in this book.

Deadly Disasters is packed with shocking tragedies, everything from fires and tornadoes to floods and plagues. And because so many people died, the book is also filled with some of the most intensely haunted places on Earth. In this spooky collection, you'll meet spirits that linger after a hurricane in Texas and a tsunami in Japan, disasters more than a century apart. They haunt deep underground in the Hoosac Tunnel and high up in the mountains of Washington State. What these ghosts have in common is that death caught them by surprise, took their lives without warning, and left their spirits trapped here on Earth, ready for you to discover.

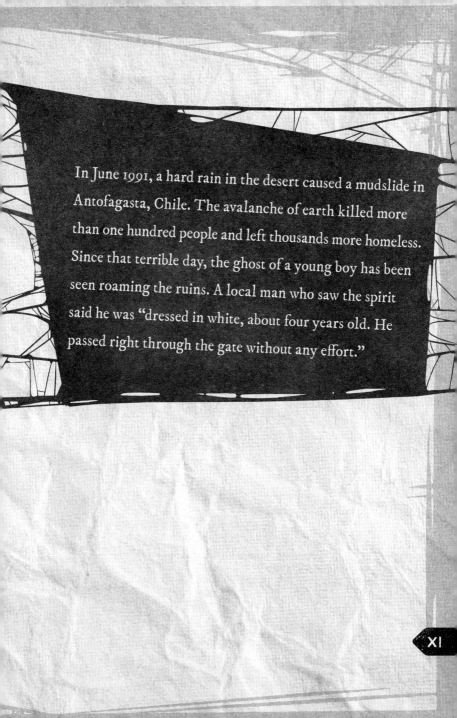

In June 1991, a hard rain in the desert caused a mudslide in Antofagasta, Chile. The avalanche of earth killed more than one hundred people and left thousands more homeless. Since that terrible day, the ghost of a young boy has been seen roaming the ruins. A local man who saw the spirit said he was "dressed in white, about four years old. He passed right through the gate without any effort."

1

"HAVE I DIED?"

2011 EARTHQUAKE AND TSUNAMI, JAPAN

The history of the Japanese port city of Ishinomaki was fairly uneventful—no big fires, no bombing during World War II, no significant damage from earthquakes. The last major disaster had been a tsunami in 869 AD, which killed more than a thousand people but happened so long ago it feels like ancient history.

That changed on March 11, 2011. At 2:46 in the afternoon, the ground began to shake. While earthquakes are fairly common in Japan, this one was huge, lasting nearly ten minutes. Warnings went out across the country that a tsunami was coming. Residents were told to leave immediately and get to higher ground. But so many of these warnings had been sent out over the years that people didn't panic.

They should have—a wave of death was heading their way.

The Japanese word "tsunami" refers to a huge sea wave caused by an earthquake or other undersea disturbance. As the wave moves inland from the sea, it builds to greater heights as the depth of the ocean decreases.

Less than a half hour later, Ishinomaki was engulfed by a massive tsunami, which flattened the town. Nearly 6,000 people were killed by the towering wave and 29,000 lost their homes. Those who survived were devastated by the damage and mourned the loss of family, friends, and neighbors.

As crushed buildings and other debris were removed from the streets and electricity was restored, the taxi services began to get some strange calls. Drivers would pick up passengers, only to have them vanish during the ride.

In one instance, a driver picked up a woman who asked to go to an area totally destroyed during the tsunami. He told her there was nothing left there to visit. "Have I died?"

she asked him. When he turned to look at her, the back seat of his taxi was empty.

☠ ☠ ☠

The island of Japan is located above underground plates that shift and collide, causing earthquakes to happen fairly often. However, the one that occurred in 2011 was anything but ordinary. Registered at 9.0 on the Richter scale, which measures the strength of earthquakes, it was the largest in Japan's history and the fourth largest in recorded history. This massive quake off the east coast was so strong it actually moved the entire country four feet closer to the United States.

While the quake was terrible, the tsunami that came less than an hour later was worse. More than 120 feet tall in places, the wave swept in from the sea and destroyed everything in its wake for nearly six miles inland.

The tsunami battered nearly 217 miles of the Pacific coast of Japan, wiping out sources for electricity, gas, and clean water. One reporter said that the wave "was mixed with mud, with ships and cars smashing toward wooden houses, dragging those into rice fields, and basically bashing them into pieces."

☠ ☠ ☠

Ryo Kanouya was inside his house when the tsunami struck. He told *National Geographic* that he thought he was going to drown when the water reached his ceiling.

The tsunami bursting into the city of Miyako.

"The next moment I heard [a] cracking sound made by my home's destruction . . . I was drained from my house into the soup of seawater, cars, houses, and everything the tsunami carried. To my surprise, I was able to reach the surface . . . Luckily a drawer for clothes came floating toward me and I climbed onto it."

Ryo and the drawer were being sucked out into the ocean with the receding wave. When he floated by a tree, Ryo held on to the branches. He stayed in the tree until the water went back out and he could climb down.

4

"When we entered the disaster area, words failed us," a man named Shunji told *Watchtower* magazine about his home in Ishinomaki. "Cars were hanging off electric poles, houses were piled one on top of the other, and the debris was piled up even higher than the houses. On the roof of a car, we saw a dead body, probably a person who was unable to survive the cold night. Another car was upside down and hanging between houses. There was a body inside it."

The earthquake and tsunami caused nearly 16,000 deaths and $220 billion in damage in Japan, as well as a nuclear disaster at the Fukushima Daiichi nuclear power station. Where were once bustling neighborhoods, there were only piles of smashed houses, stores, schools, and cars.

A man rests while digging out the rubble where his house once stood.

As people began to dig out, bury, and mourn the dead, they found that some weren't ready for their lives to be over.

While the 2011 earthquake and tsunami in Japan was devastating, it wasn't the deadliest in recorded history. The 2004 magnitude 9.1 Northern Sumatra earthquake and tsunami caused nearly 230,000 deaths and $10 billion in damage in Indonesia, Thailand, Sri Lanka, and India.

In traditional Japanese culture, ghosts are not uncommon. Some religions believe that when a person dies and their soul leaves the body, certain rituals need to be performed so that it can join its ancestors in the afterlife. If someone dies suddenly or violently or the rituals are not performed, the spirit becomes stuck on Earth. Many of these ghosts are trapped near where they died until they have been given a proper burial.

After the tsunami, a number of restless spirits were seen in the areas it had hit. Ghosts were spotted in wrecked

尾上松助

豊国画

A Japanese print from an 1812 play that featured the ghost of a murdered woman.

grocery stores and in the rubble that once was homes. Other spirits were seen running in fear as if from a wave, only to disappear. Ambulances and taxis received phantom calls from areas where no buildings were left standing.

Some who survived claimed to be approached by people they knew were dead, only to have them vanish into the air. One man saw the eyes of the many dead staring at him from rain puddles. The ghost of an old woman from Onagawa came to one of the recovery centers for tea. Those who saw her said they felt so bad for her that they didn't tell her she was dead. When she disappeared, she left behind a seat wet with seawater.

A number of the spirits, furious about their terrible deaths, were said to possess the living. Priests in the Buddhist and Shinto religions were asked to perform exorcisms, which is a ceremony that expels an evil spirit from a living person. Journalist Richard Lloyd Parry detailed how one man who had visited the area devastated by the wave became possessed. He crawled around on all fours making animal noises and rolled on the floor, yelling, "You must die. You must die. Everyone must die. Everything must die and be lost." His behavior continued to be so strange that his wife brought him to a priest, who helped rid him of the angry spirit.

Another woman couldn't escape the spirits all around

her, telling a writer, "There are headless ghosts, and some missing hands and legs. Others are completely cut in half. People were killed in so many different ways during the disaster and they were left like that in death too."

While crews gradually cleared the devastated areas of debris and the areas began to recover, many of the spirits of the thousands lost in the disaster were never put to rest. They haunt the country still.

The phone booth on the hill.

On a hill in Otsuchi, Japan, stands a white telephone booth that overlooks the Pacific Ocean. Known as "the phone of the wind" because it's not connected to any wires, it doesn't work but was created to give comfort to people who have lost someone. More than 10,000 people have visited the booth to "talk" to loved ones who died during the 2011 tsunami.

NO WAY OUT

1911 TRIANGLE SHIRTWAIST FIRE, NEW YORK

The lights in the Brown Building of Science often shine into the night with New York University students inside working late. While there is a small plaque on the building, many who go in and out of its doors every day don't realize that it is the site of a horrific tragedy—the Triangle Shirtwaist Factory Fire of 1911. But they do realize that there's something creepy about the top floors of the building.

Years after the fire, a secretary who worked at NYU reported seeing something strange there one night. As she was leaving, a woman staggered past her, looking rather dazed. She was covered in soot from a fire and didn't respond when asked if she needed help. The secretary followed the woman around a corner, only to find that she had disappeared. Was the woman one of the many victims of that awful blaze?

💀 💀 💀

When Max Blanck and Isaac Harris's Triangle Waist Company factory moved into the eighth, ninth, and tenth floors of the supposedly fireproof Asch Building in 1901, it was considered very safe and modern. Mary Domsky-Abrams, who worked on the ninth floor, later said, "The shop, both on the eighth and ninth floors, was light and airy, and was, more or less, clean, although pieces of cloth from the cutting room were strewn on the floor." All of that cloth would later prove more dangerous than it seemed.

Within the first year the company suffered two fires, both happening when no one was in the building. Each time, Blanck and Harris received a huge payment from the insurance companies for their losses. The walls of the building withstood the flames, so the company just rebuilt the interiors after each fire. Some believe that the owners never installed a sprinkler system or other fire safety equipment in the Triangle factory, in case they ever wanted another fire payout from their insurance company. That decision would come back to haunt them, literally.

By 1911, between five hundred and six hundred people worked on the factory's sewing lines and cutting floors for twelve hours a day, seven days a week. The workers were mainly immigrant teenage girls. They often didn't speak English and were paid between $6 and $15 a week, depending on their skill level.

To ensure that no workers stole from them, Blanck and Harris locked the stairway doors and had all workers use a single elevator, so their bags could be checked upon leaving.

On March 25, 1911, a small fire started on the eighth floor at around 4:45 p.m. It spread quickly among the scraps of fabric and sewing tables, which were soaked in machine oil. While someone called the tenth floor to warn them, no one alerted the nearly 260 workers on the ninth floor. The fire was now an inferno, and the workers began to fear they might not escape the flames. Rose Indursky, a sixteen-year-old who worked on the ninth floor, later said that when the fire hit, "girls were lying on the floor, fainted, and people were stepping on them. Some of the other girls were trying to climb over the machines. I remember the machinist ran to the window and he smashed it to let the smoke that was choking us go out. Instead, the flames rushed in. I stood at the window; across the street people were hollering 'don't jump, don't jump.'"

While firefighters arrived at the scene within minutes, they could do little to help. The water from their hoses and

The *"fireproof"* Asch Building in flames.

their ladders didn't reach higher than the sixth floor, so they stood there helplessly as women screamed for help from the open windows. A bystander, Frances Perkins, arrived just as desperate people began to panic. "They had been holding [on] until that time, standing in the window-sills, being crowded by others behind them, the fire pressing closer and closer, the smoke closer and closer [. . .] They began to jump. The window was too crowded and they would jump and they hit the sidewalk." They plummeted from so high that their bodies broke through the firemen's nets held out to catch them.

Other ways of escape from the fire were blocked. The stairways were locked and the flimsy fire escape ladder collapsed under the weight of the frantic women scrambling to get away. One of the only ways down was the elevator.

A worker on the ninth floor, Celia Walker Friedman, later recalled trying to find a way out. "The fire crept closer to us and we were crowded at the elevator door banging and hollering for the elevator. The first time it came up, the girls rushed in and it was crowded in a half a second. The elevator driver struggled with the door and finally closed it and went down with the screaming girls." Celia didn't make it down on that trip or the next one. "Just as I came to the door of the elevator, it dropped down right in front of me. I could hear it rush down and I was left standing on the edge trying to hold myself back from falling into the shaft . . . Behind me the girls were screaming and I could feel them pushing me more and more. I knew that in a few seconds I would be pushed into the shaft and I made a quick decision. Maybe through panic or maybe through instinct I saw the center cable of the elevator in front of me. I jumped and grabbed the cable. That is all I remember."

Celia woke in St. Vincent's Hospital, near death, with a head injury and broken arm and finger. Rescuers had found her at the bottom of the shaft. "I had saved myself by my jumping. Others had fallen down the shaft on top of me and I suppose I was found by the firemen when they were removing the dead . . . By sliding down the cable I was far enough away from where most of the bodies landed on top of the elevator cage as they fell down the shaft . . . I had a large searing scar down the middle of my body, burned by the friction of the cable which had cut through my clothing." She was one of the few who escaped that way. Dozens of people died trying to go down the elevator shaft the way that Celia did.

Some of the workers were able to scramble down the cramped stairs from the eighth floor. Sylvia Kimeldorf was one of the lucky ones. "Somebody grabbed me and another girl and pushed us through the door and hollered that we should run down and not to stop. I think that the girl right in back of me had her hair singed by flames—that's how close the fire was to us. I don't remember how I got down that narrow staircase but I was cold, wet and hysterical. I was screaming all the time," Sylvia recalled. But her horror wasn't over. When she got to the bottom, the firemen would not let her out of the building. "The bodies were falling all around us and they were afraid to let us go out because we would be killed by the falling bodies."

More than forty people died jumping to avoid the

Police covering up victims who jumped to their deaths.

flames. Reporter Charles Willis Thompson later wrote in a letter about the building's height, "It conveys no picture to the imagination to say that the fire was 100 feet above the street: figures don't make pictures. But when you stand on the street and almost topple over backward craning your neck to see a place away up in the sky, and realize the way those bodies came hurtling down over the inconceivable distance, it seems more as if it were 100 miles."

Within a half hour, the firemen had put out the flames. In that short time, 146 people had died. The city was stunned. Temporary morgues were set up so that relatives could file past to try to find their loved ones among the dead. Some were so badly burned it was hard to figure out who they were. A few weeks later, a funeral was held for those who could not be identified. More than 80,000 people came to pay their respects.

Soon after the fire, the building was repaired, including adding a number of safety features. In 1916, New York University moved into the eighth floor. By 1929, they owned the whole building.

While the building no longer houses a crowded factory, some of the fire victims are said to linger. There's a mirror on the eighth floor where students have claimed to glimpse the faces of factory workers in their reflections.

Police lining up victims of the fire in coffins for identification.

Others have seen someone falling past the windows of the upper floors out of the corners of their eyes.

Some claim to smell the occasional waft of smoke and a horrid stench of burning flesh. Doors that were locked unlock on their own, perhaps to save students from the same fate as those long-ago victims.

The Brown Building isn't the only one at NYU that is haunted. Furman Hall was built on the site of the home of horror writer Edgar Allan Poe in 1844. He wrote at least part of his famous dark poem "The Raven" there. Decades after his untimely death, his restless spirit has been seen climbing the stairs by startled law students.

WHITE DEATH

1910 WELLINGTON AVALANCHE, WASHINGTON

Stay alert when you are hiking along Iron Goat Trail on Windy Mountain! There's little to see along the old railroad tracks in the Cascade Mountains except a few abandoned buildings and the dark entrance of the old Cascade Tunnel. But hikers near Stevens Pass have heard and seen a lot of strange things on that empty mountainside.

Why is this spot considered one of the most haunted places in the state of Washington? Because it is the site of the deadliest avalanche in United States history. In 1910, a wall of snow crashed down the mountain, killing ninety-six people as they lay sleeping in a train. Since that terrible day, people have found bits of the warped wreckage and evidence of the people lost in the tragedy on the mountain.

A documentary filmmaker also captured the creepy sound of an Italian man singing at the now-empty site. Many of the train workers who perished were Italian immigrants.

The entrance to the Cascade Tunnel.

In 1910, a little snow didn't stop the Great Northern Railway's Spokane Express. A lot of snow couldn't either. Trainmaster William Harrington and his crews fought the flakes with machines specially created for the rail lines. These coal-fired rotary plows threw the snow from the tracks with giant blades. So when it began to snow on February 23, the passengers who climbed aboard the train in Spokane had no doubt that they would make it to Seattle. But many never did.

Harrington soon realized that this storm was especially terrible. The snow was piling up faster than it could be cleared, coming down at a foot per hour. One of his workers, Nyke Homonylo, marveled at its strength. "I had never seen a storm like this one, on the level was 8 to 10 feet, and in places it drifted 15 to 20 feet high."

Snow piles, filled with rocks and timber, slid from the mountain above and began covering the tracks. The Spokane Express and a mail train ultimately became stuck near the mountain town of Wellington, which mainly housed train employees. The crews worked to dig out the trains, but they weren't making headway. The snow was just too deep.

Telegraph lines were down, so there was no way to summon help. John S. Rogers later told the *Seattle Times* how the passengers nervously waited out the storm. "At Wellington we were taken care of at the hotel, where there was plenty of food for all for at least a week. To pass the time away, from Friday morning to Sunday, when we left, the crowd played cards and told stories and amused the six children who were with us," he said. "There were 12 women, and all the men put forth their best efforts to keep their spirits up, and succeeded fairly well." The crew used coal to keep the trains warm at night for sleeping, but could not determine when the tracks would be clear enough to move.

With the snow still coming down, some passengers decided to walk down the mountain rather than continue to wait, even if they were only wearing street clothes. Lawyers John Merritt and Lewis Jesseph were two who braved the cold. They hiked for four hours over twenty-foot-high snowdrifts trying to get to the town of Windy Point. Merritt later recalled spotting the Scenic Hot Springs Hotel far below them on the mountain. They sat and began to slide down the two thousand feet toward the hotel. "We could not walk; we could only slide. The wind was blowing a gale and the snow was so thick we could hardly see . . . Sliding, rolling, falling down the hill at the speed of a toboggan, we risked our lives a thousand times, as death lurked in every stone and stump that stuck up out of the snow. None of us got through without injury, but all were miraculously slight." They were the last passengers to make it successfully down the mountain before the storm worsened.

By February 26, the snow had turned to sheets of rain accompanied by thunder and lightning, making escape from the trapped trains nearly impossible for anyone else. The train's telegraph operator, William Edward Flannery, was asleep in a shack alongside the track on the night of March 1, when the storm startled him awake. "At 12:05 I woke up and saw a flash of lightning zigzag across the sky, and saw another, and then there was a loud clap of thunder," he later told newspaper reporters.

This lightning hit the mountain, which started an avalanche.

Right before snow and rock began to tumble down the

mountainside, railroad employee Charles Andrews claimed he was awoken out of a deep sleep by a ghostly voice that told him to get dressed and leave the train. He was outside just as the avalanche was unleashed. "White Death moving down the mountainside above the trains. Relentlessly it advanced, exploding, roaring, rumbling, grinding, snapping—a crescendo of sound that might have been the crashing of ten thousand freight trains," he later wrote. "It descended to the ledge where the side tracks lay, picked up cars and equipment as though they were so many

23

The twisted metal that was once the Spokane Express train.

snow-draped toys, and swallowing them up, disappeared like a white, broad monster into the ravine below."

The ten-foot wall of snow, said to be a half mile long and a quarter mile wide, quickly knocked the trains 150 feet down the mountain and buried the wreckage. For mail train conductor Ira Clary, it seemed like the end of the world had come.

"The car in which I was sleeping appeared to be picked up and tossed about like a feather," said Ira. The train rolled over and over until it finally crashed. "The mail car struck a big tree which stood in our path and popped open like an egg shell. When I realized anything I felt a sensation of suffocation and I found that I was buried six feet under the snow." Clary was lucky. He managed to dig himself out, and emerged above the wreckage.

Railroad employees rushed from buildings nearby and began pulling people out. "We got up and climbed down on the bank to where the trains had been knocked by the slide," remembered employee Flannery. "I saw a man lying on the snow and I went and got him, and put him on my back . . . and while I started up the hill, another slide hit and knocked me down underneath it, and I lost this man, I was sort of dazed and was underneath the snow some ten or 15 feet. I started to dig and climb out along the side of a tree, and finally got out." He was so stunned that he walked into the freezing river before realizing what he had done.

Many people were thrown from the train and quickly buried by the avalanche. Those not hurt worked tirelessly to drag the injured out of the snow before they suffocated. But many were trapped too deep to be found. A March 4 edition of the *San Francisco Call* wrote, "Workers searching for bodies frequently find victims by following blood stains through the snow. The melting snow had carried the stains from the mangled bodies down to the stream at the bottom of the gulch." Rescuers would find the trail of blood and dig through the snow until they found the

Avalanche blocking a snow shed.

bodies. "The snow is packed like cement and the bodies that were not mangled by the wreckage of the cars were horribly crushed by the weight of the icy mass."

Ninety-six men, women, and children were killed by the avalanche, the deadliest in United States history. The bodies were buried so deeply, some as much as forty feet, that it took until the end of July for the last to be dug out. Men dragged the wrapped bodies on sleds to the Scenic Hot Springs Hotel in Windy Point. Once the tracks were cleared, they were then taken by train to Everett and Seattle.

The dead being transported by sled to Windy Point.

Soon after the tragedy, the town was renamed Tye, after the nearby river. However, it was abandoned in 1929 after a new tunnel was built lower on the mountain.

While the track is now a hiking trail, the horrible history of Wellington remains. Some who make the trek have heard bodiless voices inside the railroad tunnel. Cold spots appear suddenly, even on warm days. Others have claimed to see people appear, then suddenly vanish along the tracks. Even more have been touched by unseen hands.

One ghost hunter who investigated the claims recorded an electronic voice phenomenon of someone yelling, "Avalanche, get out!" If only the sleeping train passengers had heard it in 1910!

West of Wellington is the town of Snohomish, home to the Oxford Saloon, which was built in the 1900s. After a card game there one night, a fight broke out. A policeman tried to stop it and was stabbed to death. His ghost has been seen repeatedly in the basement, including in photos taken by ghost hunters.

TORNADO ALLEY

1908 ALBERTVILLE TORNADO, ALABAMA

Albertville, Alabama, sits smack dab in the middle of one of the worst tornado alleys in the country. While these huge columns of spinning winds are always frightening, none were as terrifying as the one that hit on April 24, 1908.

Slicing into the area at approximately 4:00 in the afternoon, the massive tornado was the worst the town had ever seen. J. W. Nash, who lived nearby, later told reporters, "I looked and beheld one of the grandest sights, in its awfulness, I ever looked on in my life. A great cloud funnel shaped, with the small end dragging the ground, and the large end reached far up in the heavens." It left a five-mile path of destruction in the town, killing fifteen people and leaving nearly 1,250 homeless.

One of the few photos of a tornado funnel from that time, this one in Kansas in 1913.

Among the dead were a number of children, one of whom is said to haunt Main Street. In the years since, a little boy wearing a white shirt and tan suspenders has been seen playing downtown. Observers say he sometimes darts into the street, causing cars to screech to a halt. Then he runs away, giggling.

☠ ☠ ☠

For two days, starting on April 23, 1908, at least thirty-four tornadoes touched down across the southern United States, killing more than 320 people. On the second day, the one that hit northern Alabama at around 2:40 p.m. traveled 125 miles toward Albertville during the next hour and a half.

"A funnel-shaped cloud swept along the entire path of the storm," a weather reporter wrote of the terrible force. "The cloud is reported to have had a bounding and whirling motion, and said to have swept everything from its path where it touched the ground. A loud, rumbling noise was heard from the cloud, which emitted brilliant lightning."

As the tornado barreled toward Albertville, there was little warning of its approach. The afternoon sky suddenly grew dark, and jagged hail fell. People quickly ran for cover when the tornado landed north of the train depot at 4:00 p.m.

The devastated town of Albertville after being hit by a tornado.

The winds were so strong that they blew boxcars off the railroad tracks and destroyed any buildings in their path. As the tornado moved through town, the writhing column leveled stores and homes. A nine-ton oil tank was ripped from its fastenings and blown a half mile away.

T. W. Robertson was going into a feed store when it reached town. The tornado whipped him into the air, over trees and houses, dropping him a quarter mile away, bruised and with a broken arm. Another townsperson, Ben Phillip, was pulled out of a pasture and deposited on top of an outhouse.

John Decker and four of his children were seriously injured by the winds and falling debris. His wife, Fannie, and two other children suffered a much worse fate. The *Gadsden Daily Times News* wrote, "In one room, lay the mother, dead, clasping to her bosom the body of a little child one year old, which she tried vainly to shield." His three-year-old daughter was also dead near her amid the rubble.

The Albertville mayor's wife, Rena McCord, and her five children tried to find shelter. Sixteen-year-old Eric McCord hid under the house, only to die when the wind caused the building to collapse on him. His youngest sibling was far luckier, getting trapped beneath the opening behind a piano, which ended up saving the child. Rena was injured, as was another McCord child, who ended up losing two toes.

"I have never seen anything like it," a nearby towns-person later wrote to the governor, regarding the destruction. "So complete and absolute as to leave little of worth in the path of the storm through town. On viewing the wreckage, covering easily forty acres or more in the heart of town, it appears incredible that any living being could have escaped the fury of the storm and death." Downtown was demolished, with homes reduced to piles of broken boards and trees twisted off at the stumps. The only building not leveled was the train depot.

Within hours, surrounding towns responded to tele-grams filled with pleas for help by sending doctors and

Debris in Albertville where there used to be houses.

nurses to care for the hundreds injured. Everyone pitched in, including the head of the local militia, who had left his post only once, to bury his mother. Over time, the town was rebuilt and grew. But the spirits of those lost in the storm linger.

The Memory Hill Cemetery houses the graves of a number of those killed by the tornado, including Eric McCord and Fannie Decker. Ghosts have been spotted there, including a female spirit who is said to eerily hum the song "Amazing Grace."

Exactly 102 years after that devastation, a tornado struck Albertville again. Homes, businesses, and schools were extensively damaged. Luckily, no one was killed, so no new ghosts haunt the town.

On May 20, 2013, a tornado tore through Moore, Oklahoma. Nine-year-old Nicolas McCabe was one of seven children killed at Plaza Towers Elementary School that day. The following Fourth of July, his father took a photo of Nicolas's cousin, his niece. Behind her head was the ghostly image of Nicolas, celebrating one of his favorite holidays.

5

IROQUOIS INFERNO

1903 IROQUOIS THEATER FIRE, ILLINOIS

Nellie Reed.

Nellie Reed was a member of the Flying Ballet, one of the most exciting jobs in theater. An aerialist, she was trained to "fly" above the audience during plays (actually hanging from a thin steel wire). On December 30, 1903, she was one of the cast of 250 in the musical *Mr. Bluebeard* at the Iroquois Theater in Chicago. Her job was to sail above the audience and shower them with pink carnations. But during this fateful performance, she never made her entrance.

A fire broke out in the theater that night and quickly spread. Some say she was trapped above the stage by the flames and fell, later dying from her injuries. So many people were killed that it was hard to identify all the bodies. But Nellie's ghost is now said to haunt the theater. She often appears as a silhouette in a white tutu against the wall behind the theater, in what became known after the tragedy as "Death Alley."

The Iroquois Theater before the fire.

Lucky kids on Christmas break found themselves at the snazzy new Iroquois Theater on that cold afternoon. They had come to see popular comedian Eddie Foy appearing in *Mr. Bluebeard.* Nearly two thousand people, mainly women and children, crowded the three levels of Wednesday's standing-room-only matinee.

When the second act began with the song "The Pale Moonlight," few theatergoers noticed that a stage light threw sparks. This caused a small flame to quickly shoot up the set. Only after it had raced toward the ceiling, catching on to the scenery that hung there, did the performers onstage become concerned. They continued dancing

The scene onstage when the fire started. The X in the photo shows where the fire began.

along to the orchestra playing, nervously watching the stagehands rush around trying to put the fire out.

Glowing embers began to rain down on the dancers, alerting the audience of the danger. Eddie Foy rushed to the front of the stage to calm the crowds, who had started to rush frantically toward the exits. Foy managed to soothe them until the ropes holding the burning scenery gave way, causing it to plummet to the stage. "The fire seemed to spread with a series of explosions," Eddie later said. "The paint on the curtains and scenery came in touch with the flames and in a second the scenery was sputtering and blazing up on all sides. The smoke was fearful and it was a case of run quickly or be smothered."

The stagehands tried to lower the stage's fire curtain, which would have blocked the blaze from reaching the audience. However, the curtain malfunctioned, stopping before it reached the stage. Performers, fleeing from the flames, burst through the doors backstage to get out of the theater. This caused a gust of wind, which pushed a wave of blistering fire out into the theater. The crowd ran from the heat. Theatergoer Frank Houseman later recalled trying to escape: "There was a blast of flame or fire, a sort of ball or something that appeared to me like it was a lot of scenery that was burning down, scenery or flimsy work. It burnt a great deal on the order of paper. All I thought of was the opening of that door, because the people at that time were crowding close to me and screaming and hallooing. I don't just remember just how I got that door open, but anyway it opened and carried the crowd out." Others were not so lucky.

The lights went out, darkening the doors, windows, hallways, and fire escapes, increasing the crowd's panic. Every open space immediately became jammed with people, fighting to get free. In the awful chaos, mothers were torn from their children and husbands from their wives. Many people who tripped in the dark were thrown to the floor and trampled to death.

Some exits could not open with the crush of people

Police measuring one of the theater exits where people became crushed during the fire.

against the doors; others were locked or hidden by curtains. The building flues—chimneys that were built to direct fire away from the crowds—had been barred and grated, making them useless. While the walls and floors of the building were fireproof, the seat tops, rail cushions, and wall decorations provided plenty of fuel. The fire quickly spread.

"The stampede that followed the first alarm, a struggle in which most contestants were women and children, fighting with the desperation of death, terminated with the sudden sweep of the sea of flames across the body of the house. Somehow those on the main floor managed to force their way out," witness Ben Atwell later wrote. However, those on the upper floors could not escape. "The wave of flame, smoke and gas smote the multitude. Dropping where they stood,

Victims of the fire lined the sidewalk in front of the theater.

most of the victims were consumed beyond recognition."

James McGurn was attending a play down the street when he heard the Iroquois's fire alarm. He rushed over to help and saw two men charging upstairs, past some firemen in the lobby. He said, "I was watching the stairs, and they were up there thirty seconds, about, when the fireman came down with the first body, a little girl, about eight years old. He shouted out to the firemen, 'For God's sake to get up there.' All the firemen I saw in the lobby dropped everything and went up, and they weren't up there but a few seconds before they came tumbling down with bodies, and after I had remained there about three minutes more I saw dozens of bodies brought down."

A woman searching for her children among the dead.

Police Chief Francis O'Neill was quickly on the scene. He later wrote, "In the rush for the stairs [people] had jammed in the doorway and piled ten deep; lying almost like shingles. When we got up the stairs in the dark to the front rows of the victims, some of them were alive and struggling, but so pinned down by the great weight of the dead and dying piled upon them that three strong men could not pull the unfortunate ones free ... It was necessary first to take the dead from the top of the pile, then the rest of the bodies were lifted easily and regularly from their positions, save as their arms had intertwined and clutched." In less than twenty minutes, nearly six hundred people— mostly women and children—died, some from the flames, some from the smoke, and others from being crushed by those trying to escape.

A number of people on the top floors were able to get out using the exits that led to Couch Place behind the theater. The fire escape was narrow and icy but would have been a way to escape if the doors on the lower floors hadn't blocked the walkway when they opened. People on the third floor couldn't get past them. Painters working on a neighboring building saw the trapped people. They pushed a ladder and then planks over to the fire escape to help some crawl to safety. But they couldn't save many. Others fell or were pushed by the crowds to their deaths.

Nearly 125 people died there, giving rise to the name "Death Alley."

Some of those who owned and operated the theater were arrested, but no one was ever prosecuted for the lack of safety features that caused so many deaths that day. The theater was rebuilt and stayed in business until 1924. It was demolished and another theater was built in its place, but the alley remains.

People who have traveled this cursed passageway claim to hear faint cries and a child giggling. In the heat of the summer, they feel cold spots. Others have taken photos of the empty alley only to have ghostlike figures appear in their images.

Chicago's most famous ghost is Resurrection Mary, a young woman in a white dress with blond hair and blue eyes. Since the 1930s, she has been known to meet a man at a local ballroom, dance the night away with him, then, as he drives her home, vanish in front of the gates of the Resurrection Cemetery on Archer Avenue. At the spot where she disappears, the gates appear to have been pried open and handprints seared into the metal.

A HEADLESS HAUNTING

6

1900 SCOFIELD MINE, UTAH

Thomas J. Parmley was superintendent of Winter Quarters, one of the biggest, safest, and most productive coal mines in Utah. And Tuesday, May 1, 1900, was the worst day of his life. At 10:28 in the morning, there was an explosion in Mine 4 that was so strong it shook the ground. Men and boys ran from the smoke and debris pouring from the entrance, as well as from Mine 1, which was connected underground to Mine 4.

Thomas immediately called the mine owners at Pleasant Valley Coal Company to alert them to the trouble. He then gathered together a search party of about twenty men. As the entrance to Mine 4 was blocked by twisted coal cars and dead horses, he led the men to Mine 1.

Thomas Parmley, center, talking with mine workers in the aftermath of the explosion.

They quickly found three badly burned men, who they carried out. This was the beginning of weeks of rescue and recovery.

Resting one day after the exhausting search, Thomas got a knock on his door. A ten-year-old boy was there to ask if Thomas would go back into the damaged mine and get his father's body. His ghost had been visiting the boy every night in a dream, saying he couldn't rest until he had been properly buried. The boy insisted that his father was in the parish No. 12 section of the mine.

When the recovery crew were finally able to reach that part of the massive mine, the body was exactly where the boy said it would be.

The disaster that rocked Mine 4 started with an underground explosion. This ignited the coal dust that coated the mine, sending flames that sounded like rolling thunder racing through the tunnels. As miners ran to the exits, many were struck dead by "afterdamp."

Afterdamp is a combination of poisonous gases that occurs after an explosion in a mine. The carbon monoxide left after the flames suffocates victims by depriving their lungs of oxygen. Before gas detectors were invented, canaries were kept in mines as a warning system for afterdamp. The small birds were more sensitive to afterdamp than humans, so if they died, it meant miners should get out because there were dangerous gases in the mine.

Few survived the terrible blast. James Naylor, who was near the mine entrance, was blown two hundred feet in the air but wasn't severely injured. John Wilson, who was thrown 820 feet, was not as lucky. He was found with a crushed skull and a branch sticking out of his stomach.

Evan Williams and James Naylor, who survived the mine explosion.

John was taken to the hospital and miraculously recovered. But he was one of the few. While rescue efforts were immediate, for many of the more than three hundred men and boys, it was already too late.

Even some who survived the initial explosion weren't entirely safe. Walter Clark escaped the mine and quickly joined the rescue party, determined to find his brothers William and George, who had not made it out. He raced ahead of the other men, only to run right into the after-damp from the explosion. He died soon after.

John James and his son were trying to escape when "the deadly damp overtook them, and a moment later they were dead," wrote a reporter at the time. "When found by the rescuers, their arms were tightly clasped about each other in an embrace that death could not loosen."

"We had some hard experiences today going through the mine," one man from the rescue party said, describing to reporters what they found. "Several times, members of our party were overcome by the damp, but we got them out in time. We found bodies of the men in every conceivable shape, but generally they were lying on their stomachs with their arms about their faces. The men died almost instantly when struck by the damp and did not suffer. They

A widow and her seven orphaned children after their father died in the mine.

just became unconscious and were asphyxiated. Their faces were all calm and peaceful as though they had just fallen asleep."

The *Deseret News* reported on the sad aftermath of the tragedy, "The removal of the bodies from the mine was begun at noon yesterday, hundreds of men having volunteered their services for the purpose. These rescuers came from other mines and towns surrounding and worked incessantly to bring out the burnt and mangled remains of the dead miners . . . Many of the rescuers came near losing their lives from the fatal afterdamp, but the work was continued in the face of all danger, and most of the brave fellows remained at their posts until they were almost ready to drop."

Bodies being taken by train from the temporary morgue at the boardinghouse into the town of Scofield.

The bodies were taken to makeshift morgues set up in the boardinghouses, churches, and schools in town.

News of the disaster spread quickly, with mine owners arriving from Salt Lake City the next day, anxious to help. They were soon followed by a train that, when it was opened, was found to be filled with flowers. Salt Lake City schoolchildren had heard about the explosion and collected flowers to cover the coffins of the dead.

And there were so many coffins. The disaster at Scofield used all the coffins that could be found in Utah,

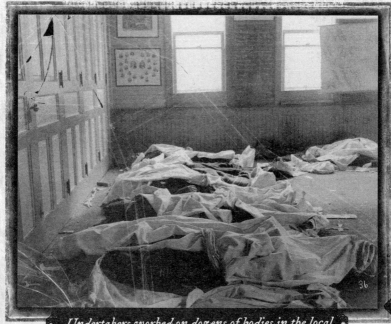

Undertakers worked on dozens of bodies in the local school, trying to get them ready to be buried.

with another seventy-five shipped from Denver, Colorado. More than two hundred men and boys were killed, many recent immigrants, leaving more than one hundred widows and nearly three hundred orphans. As many as 125 of the miners were buried in Scofield, the rest taken by funeral train to their hometowns. The *Deseret News* reported, "Every house, without exception, is a house of mourning and every household is preparing to receive its dead. The awful scene of yesterday had passed away when the day dawned this morning and the awful calm of despair had taken its place." At the time, it was the worst mining disaster in United States history.

The family of miner Levi Jones grieving around his coffin.

The mine reopened twenty-eight days after the explosion. Many who lived through that awful day swore they would never step foot into the mine again, but eventually ended up going back to work. From the moment they returned, they were literally haunted by the spirits of those who were killed. Miners heard ghostly voices and agonized groans, as well as saw strange blue lights in the cemetery thought to be spirits trapped on Earth.

Soon after, the miners were visited by a ghost they recognized. A 1901 article in the *Anaconda Standard* wrote, "From what these men said it appears that the ghost was in the form of a miner without a head. The men state positively that they saw this headless ghost and declared that they would not work another second in the place." The ghost was soon identified as the spirit of Sandy McGovern, a miner whose body was the last to be taken out of the fatal pit after the explosion following several days of searching. He sometimes appeared in coal cars carrying miners out of the mine, sitting quietly until the wagon hit daylight, then disappearing.

The mines continued operating for another thirty years. Once they closed, Winter Quarters and Scofield gradually became ghost towns, empty but for the remaining spirits.

The Morfa Colliery, a mine in South Wales, had many explosions in its history, including one in 1863 where thirty men were killed and another in 1870 that killed thirty. However, the worst blast was yet to come. Leading up to an explosion in 1890, miners were said to have heard sounds and signs from spirits that they were in danger. These included the ghost of a pitman and the strange smell of roses and honeysuckle. Of the 250 men working deep underground that terrible day, eighty-seven were killed. Some of their bodies were never recovered, leading to even more hauntings. Five years after the explosion, workers were so frightened by wailing and knocking in the dark mines that they threw down their tools and refused to go back to work.

THE LITTLE GHOSTS OF GALVESTON

1900 GALVESTON FLOOD, TEXAS

From the back of the Galveston Walmart, an employee heard a child crying, calling for her mom. She searched up and down the aisles, asking other employees and customers to help. They all heard the quiet sobbing and it always sounded like the child was close by. But every aisle she searched was empty.

Maybe the employee wasn't looking in the wrong place, but in the wrong time. To find the terrified child, she needed to be on that site on September 8, 1900, the date of the worst national disaster in United States history.

The Walmart is built where St. Mary's Orphan Asylum once stood. In 1900, the two-story buildings of the asylum were beachfront property, standing behind tall dunes on the island, west of the center of town. They were home to ninety-three children who had lost their parents.

They were cared for by ten Sisters of Charity of the Incarnate Word, a French order of the Catholic Church.

When it started to rain on the morning of September 8, 1900, the city of Galveston considered it simply an inconvenient storm. The rich seaside home of 36,000 people had never seen much damage from the weather. But that day the rain was actually the beginnings of a massive

The boys' and girls' dormitories at St. Mary's Orphan Asylum.

hurricane. By 5:00 p.m., the winds reached 130–140 miles per hour, causing ten-foot-high waves to crash over the dunes on the gulf side and push water in from the bay side as well. As no part of the island was higher than nine feet above sea level, buildings quickly began to flood. The winds knocked down electricity and telegraph lines, plunging the city into darkness and making it impossible to telegraph for help. By the time people understood the danger they were in, it was too late to evacuate.

F. T. Woodward was among a crowd huddled in Galveston's Grand Central Station when the storm hit. As he sheltered there, the strong winds burst in all the windows. "The crashing of glass was soon followed by a sound of ripping and tearing," he later wrote. "Section after section of the tin roof was rolled up like sheets of parchment and hurled hundreds of feet away. To add to the terror and confusion, the electric lights suddenly went out and the building was left in darkness, except where the trainmen with their lanterns stood . . . Nearer and nearer came that awful rumbling. A shower of brick and mortar fell in the rear of the women's waiting-room. Nothing remained of the tin-covered awning. Few, if any, doubted that the end had come and that in another moment all would be buried beneath the ruins."

A hurricane is a severe tropical cyclone with wind speeds of seventy-four miles per hour or more. Hurricanes are categorized by numbers 1 to 5, with Category 1 being the weakest. The Galveston Hurricane is considered a Category 4, which has winds of 130–156 mph.

Within St. Mary's Orphan Asylum, fierce winds caused the building to groan. Water began to pour into the first floor. Moving the children upstairs in the girls' dormitory, the nuns helped calm the frightened children by singing a hymn, "Queen of the Waves," which sailors sang during storms:

> Queen of the Waves, look forth across the ocean
> See how the waters with tumultuous motion
> Rise up and foam without a pause or rest.
> Help, then sweet Queen, in our exceeding danger,
> . . . help us now, dear Lady of the Wave

Frank Madera, a twelve-year-old orphan who lived through the storm, later told a newspaper, "We were terrified, and the sisters had much trouble with the younger children. I must say there was never a braver group of women. They comforted the smallest ones, some not more than 2 years old, as best they could."

William Murney, aged thirteen, held on to his little brother, Joe, who was eight. They had been at St. Mary's a few years, after their mother died of tuberculosis and their father of a heart attack within days of each other.

William Murney, who was age thirteen at the time of the hurricane.

At around 7:00 p.m., the main tidal surge of the storm hit Galveston, sending a fifteen-to-twenty-foot wall of water into the city, pulling trees, boats, and buildings in its wake. At the asylum, the children grew terrified as they heard the boys' dormitory next door collapse.

In the darkness, the sisters had a workman collect all of the clotheslines in the building. Each sister then began tying six to eight children to the belts they wore around their waists. Albert Campbell, aged thirteen, later wrote that one sister promised two small children she would not let them go. "She said they would stay together, no matter what."

Sister Vincent Cottier and two orphans.

Some older children climbed out the windows. Albert wrote, "I saw boys and girls on the roof. I also remember one of the men at the home having a baby on his back. But it washed off."

The water kept rising in the dormitory. "The building began to float," Frank remembered. "I don't know how far out in the gulf we floated . . . Then suddenly something crashed into us and one wall caved in. The children and the grown-ups didn't have a chance. The floor sank as a great wave hit . . ." William Murney was hit by a falling timber and lost hold of his brother, Joe, who he never saw again. The building collapsed, burying many of the children and sisters in the rubble.

Frank, William, and Albert were able to swim to a tree that had been caught in the mast of a wrecked boat. At one point Albert thought he was going to drown, so William tied him to the tree with a piece of rope he found. The three boys floated for more than a day before the waters receded. They were picked up by a man in a small boat and returned to town, now the scene of the country's most terrible natural disaster. Nearly 8,000 people were dead and 3,600 buildings were destroyed.

"Great piles of human bodies, dead animals, rotting vegetation, household furniture, and fragments of the houses themselves are piled in confused heaps right in the main streets of the city," wrote Henry Wortham of the destruction. "Along the gulf front human bodies are floating around like cordwood. Intermingled with them are to be found the carcasses of horses, chickens, dogs, and rotting vegetable matter. Above all arises the foulest stench . . . absolutely sickening in its intensity and most dangerous to health in its effects."

The next day, rescuers scoured the city, trying to find anyone still alive. Amid the rubble, they found the body of

Relief party looking for survivors amid the destroyed buildings.

a child in the sand near where St. Mary's had been. Lifting it, they found the corpse was attached by a rope around the wrist to another child, and that child to another. At the end was one of the sisters, who stayed with her orphans until the end. About ten miles away, the body of another sister was found, still holding two lifeless little bodies. In total, ninety children and ten sisters from the orphanage died. Only the three boys survived.

Each year on September 8, the members of the congregation of the Sisters of Charity of the Incarnate Word around the world sing "Queen of the Waves" to pay tribute to the sisters and children who lost their lives on that horrible day.

The three-mile-long, thirty-foot-high piles of debris that were once the city of Galveston took more than a year to clean up. St. Mary's Orphan Asylum was reopened in a new location in 1901. On the anniversary of the storm in 1994, a marker was placed in the location where the asylum once stood, along the seawall built to protect the city from any future storms.

When a Walmart was built on the site of the asylum many years later, employees began noticing something strange. Toys would be found missing or misplaced, and the sound of children running up and down the aisles was heard when the store was empty. A small girl's voice has been heard calling for her mother.

In 2008, Hurricane Ike struck and flooded the Walmart. Rescue workers were allowed inside the store to get supplies. While gathering what they could from the damaged store, they heard children laughing and coughing. They searched the entire store, but didn't find any evidence of living children in the building.

Another haunting occurs near where the bodies of a nun and the children she was tied to were discovered after the storm. Like many of those killed, they were buried where they were found. In 1911, the grand Hotel Galvez was built over their graves.

Some say that when a big storm is approaching, a nun can be seen worriedly pacing the shore in front of the hotel. Children have also been heard running through the halls and opening and closing doors. Could it be the orphans lost in the storm so many years ago?

Even those who didn't die are still haunted by the storm. When survivor Frank Madera was interviewed decades later, he said, "I go wild when it storms. Not that I'm afraid to die—not that. But I can't sleep, and I think of those who might be in the storm. I hear just one terrible, solid scream of 100 children."

Hotel Galvez is thought to be haunted by the victims of the hurricane.

When a hurricane is set to hit Pawleys Island, South Carolina, residents often keep an eye out for the Gray Man. The ghost was first seen in 1822 and is said to appear on the beach to warn residents when a deadly storm is approaching. He has been seen before every major hurricane, and those who heed his warning are said to be spared from the worst of the storms.

GHOST TRAIN NO. 9

8

1891 BOSTIAN BRIDGE TRAIN WRECK, NORTH CAROLINA

On the first anniversary of North Carolina's deadliest train crash, the train's baggage master, Hugh Leinster, was seen checking his watch close to the Bostian Bridge near Statesville. He lived in Statesville and had worked for the railroad for years, most recently on the Ashville-bound line in North Carolina.

Looking sharp in his uniform, Leinster appeared worried the train was late again, just like the night of the crash. But those who saw him that night will never know for sure what was wrong. Because Hugh Leinster is dead. He was one of the first killed when the No. 9 train hit the ground the year before.

When the train rolled into the Statesville station past midnight on August 27, 1891, it was already behind schedule. Passengers boarded quickly and soon it was back on the tracks heading west.

Two miles into the run, the train neared the Bostian Bridge going about thirty miles per hour. As it crossed the sixty-foot-high span, the wheels started bumping and jerking. Seven cars in the back suddenly derailed from the track. There was barely time to scream before the train plummeted from the bridge, falling through the pitch-dark into the creek below.

Statesville Station in North Carolina.

Marshall Nix, a fireman traveling to Asheville, remembered feeling a jolt and told the *Asheville Daily Citizen*, "I felt the horrible sensation of going downward, I knew not where. In a twinkling, however the crash had come. It was an instant but seemed like an age ... The noise of the engine for a short while drowned out all other sound ... the noise from the engine ceased and I could hear the heartrending cries of the wounded.

"The most horrible sounds I ever heard greeted my ears: 'Lord help me!' 'Oh God, have mercy' 'Let me up!'

The No. 9 train jumping the tracks.

'I am dying, water, water.' And every imaginable cry, shriek, and wail of distress was borne out on the air, enough to make the stoutest heart fail and sicken."

At least twenty people were killed immediately when the train hit the ground. Others became trapped in the high water of the creek, which rose steadily as the flow was held back by the crash. Luella Pool, who survived the initial impact, desperately tried to hold her mother's head above the water for as long as she could. But she was injured and weak, and eventually had to let go. She helplessly watched as her mother drowned beside her.

Orville Lawson, a twenty-three-year-old salesman, was traveling with George Bowly when the train jumped the tracks. They survived the fall but Lawson later said in a newspaper interview, "by that time the groans of the injured had begun to swell into a veritable discord and after three or four attempts I was able to get through the window. In a moment Bowly followed me. [We] both were so badly hurt that blood was flowing freely from several cuts, one of mine being an artery at the left side of my face, and which gave me much concern," he said. "Bowly asked if I could wait until he looked at the engine. When he came back, he said both the engineman and the fireman were dead, and we decided we were not strong enough to

The train lying crushed below the Bostian Bridge.

undertake relief work, but had best get to someone who was able and send help in numbers with bandages."

A number of passengers who, like Lawson and Bowly, weren't badly hurt, began walking back to Statesville to get help. There was no ambulance or hospital in town, so townspeople rushed back to aid the wounded and pull bodies from the wreckage. In total, twenty-two people died and more than thirty were seriously injured. The dead were taken to be stored in the Farmers' Tobacco Warehouse. Those who couldn't be moved were cared for at private houses nearby, with others carried by wagon to hotels in town.

A doctor on the train who had just graduated medical

school helped, as well as the Statesville doctor, who came to the aid of Orville Lawson. "I refused morphine when he took those seventeen stitches in me," he said. He eventually fell asleep, exhausted from his ordeal. "When I wakened later, I saw a young man sitting by my bed with a peach tree brush keeping flies from my wounds and blood stained clothing. I looked at him and he smiled. I tried to grin but the stitches reminded me by protesting."

Just days after the horrible crash, the tracks were repaired and trains began crossing it again. Everything on

The twisted wreck of the No. 9 train.

the bridge seemed to return to normal. Until exactly one year later, when Hugh Leinster was seen again at the crash site, checking his watch. This marked the beginning of years of ghost sightings.

In 1897, the railroad company finally determined the cause of the crash. Two inmates in the state prison, J. A. Hand and Bird Shepherd, had bragged about taking large spikes out of the rails that held the cross ties on the bridge before they were imprisoned. This was what caused the train to derail, so the men were charged with murder. While some justice was served, it didn't stop the hauntings.

On the night of the fiftieth anniversary of the tragedy, Pat Hayes and her husband were driving along a road by the bridge when their car broke down. Pat waited with the car while her husband walked back to town to get help.

Suddenly, the phantom form of the No. 9 train appeared, barreling along the bridge, and, as she watched in horror, plunged into the creek. Not long after, a baggage man approached the shell-shocked Pat, asked her for the time, then faded into the night. As she was not local, she had no idea about the area's dark history. She didn't realize the crash she had seen was decades old until she reached Statesville the next morning.

After news of the haunting spread beyond Statesville, people began to come every year on August 27 to the

Cars along a North Carolina highway at night.

Bostian Bridge and wait late into the night, hoping to catch a glimpse of the ghost train. On the one hundredth anniversary, more than 150 people were there and locals were selling T-shirts. But the apparition did not appear.

However, the 119th anniversary made news. That night at 3:00 a.m., more than a dozen ghost hunters were sitting in the middle of the bridge when they saw a light coming down the track. But it wasn't a ghost train. A real Norfolk Southern train, with an engine and three cars, was heading toward them. They ran, trying to make it across the 150 feet of bridge to safety. Almost all were successful, except

Christopher Kaiser, a twenty-eight-year-old who had grown up in the area hearing stories of the No. 9. While the engineer blew the horn and threw on the brake, the train was going too fast to stop. Kaiser was able to push a girl out of the way before he was struck by the train and killed.

Bobbing lights have often been seen along the train tracks near North Carolina's Maco train station. When someone gets close, the lights disappear. Local legend claims it is the ghost of a railroad worker, Joe Baldwin, who was decapitated trying to stop an accident caused by a runaway train in 1867. His headless ghost is thought to be the source of the lights, warning people off the tracks.

THE BLOODY PIT

9

1860 HOOSAC TUNNEL, MASSACHUSETTS

In order to construct the 4.75-mile-long Hoosac Tunnel, nearly two million tons of rock were taken out of the Berkshire mountain range. Most of this dangerous work was done by hand. Between falling rocks, accidental explosions, and deadly gas, nearly two hundred men were killed in the twenty years it took to build the tunnel, earning it the terrible nickname "The Bloody Pit."

With so much death in its short history, it wasn't long before Hoosac became haunted. Workers claimed to hear the dead moaning in the dark. In 1868, a mechanical engineer, Paul Travers, went to inspect the tunnel. Having fought in the Civil War, he wasn't easily spooked. But in a letter later written to his sister, he described a night inspection he and a worker named Mr. Dunn made that terrified him.

"We traveled about two miles into the shaft and then we stopped to listen. As we stood there in the cold silence, we both heard what truly sounded like a man groaning out in pain. As you know, I have heard this same sound many times during the war. Yet, when we turned up the wicks on our lamps, there were no other human beings in the shaft except Mr. Dunn and myself. I'll admit I haven't been this frightened since [the Battle of] Shiloh. Mr. Dunn agreed that it wasn't the wind we heard."

At a time when the invention of the light bulb was still more than twenty years away, workers for the Troy and Greenfield Railroad in Massachusetts were attempting to do what many thought was impossible. They planned on digging a tunnel through a Berkshire mountain so that trains could more easily reach stations in the west. In 1851, millions of dollars were paid and hundreds of workers hired to begin the backbreaking work of excavating the rock. They dug holes by hand with pickaxes, packed them full of black powder, similar to gunpowder, blew them up, then dug out the blasted rock. But this early chemical explosive wasn't very strong, so progress was slow.

That changed when the first nitroglycerin factory in

the country was built near the tunnel. While this new, more powerful explosive made the dig go faster, it also made it far more deadly. Miners were just learning how to use nitroglycerin. Every mistake could mean death.

In December 1870, the nitroglycerin factory itself blew up. A newspaper story from the time described "a tremendous report, shattering the magazine and blowing to atoms the foreman in charge—John V. Velsor. Mr. Velsor was literally blown to pieces and scattered in all directions. Not a fragment of the body as large as the hand was found, but only small pieces of flesh and bone, picked up here and there on the ground and in the branches of trees, where they had been blown."

Workers drilling in the Hoosac Tunnel in 1865.

In another accident, a miner named Ringo Kelley accidentally lit nitroglycerin before fellow miners Ned Brinkman and Billy Nash could run for cover. They were killed instantly. Not long after, Ringo Kelley was found strangled to death in the exact spot where the men had died. Many workers thought his murder was the revenge of the men's ghosts.

Most of the rock was taken out of the mountain by the workers by hand.

Nitroglycerin, invented in 1847, was used in the manufacture of explosives, most often in dynamite. It was dangerous to transport. After a crate of nitroglycerin exploded in San Francisco, killing fifteen people, safety regulations required that it be manufactured where it was being used. That is why a factory was built near the Hoosac Tunnel.

And nitroglycerin wasn't the only danger for Hoosac workers. The Central Shaft, which allowed air into the tunnel, was 1,058 feet deep. In 1867, a local paper reported one of the many times this drop turned deadly. "Fred Trombley, a Frenchman, who worked at the bottom of the Central Shaft, was fatally injured by the falling of an iron drill from the top of the shaft. This drill, by some cause unknown, fell point down 325 feet and struck Trombley in the abdomen. It passed through his bowels and came out below the knee and pierced a two inch plank on which he was standing, thus pinning him to the ground." He, not surprisingly, died shortly after.

Miners descending into the tunnel to work.

In 1873, a man fell down the deep shaft himself. "It is said that when the body of this man reached the bottom, while the skin was perfectly whole, every bone was broken; the corpse was so limber that it could be rolled up like a side of leather."

The worst accident in the shaft occurred in 1867, when gas caught fire, burning a water-pumping station built at the top of the shaft. All the flaming equipment in the station rained down the pit and onto the thirteen men working more than one thousand feet below. With the pumping station on fire, water began filling the shaft. A large bucket was lowered to try to rescue the men, but the flames burned through the connections holding it up. The bucket plunged to the bottom, knocking a number of drills on platforms along the edge of the shaft onto the men.

Once the fire at the top of the shaft was put out, a brave man named Thomas Mallory offered to be lowered into the fume-filled shaft to see if anyone was still alive.

"Hundreds of people surrounded the scene, among whom were the trembling families of three of the miners," a newspaper later wrote of the tense descent. "The dense crowd hushed into silence and awaited the result with

Thomas Mallory descending into the shaft to see if any miners survived.

agonizing suspense ... The fate of the miners hung in the balance. The time seemed terribly long—twenty, thirty, forty minutes elapsed when the signal came from below. Mallory was drawn up and had only time to say that there was no hope when he fainted ... He had gone to the bottom only to see the shaft covered with water to a depth of 10 or 15 feet and the burned timbers and brands floating on the surface, but found no trace of the unfortunate men." The gas fumes were too thick to make another attempt at rescue. All men were thought to be killed from either being crushed by the burning equipment or suffocated by the fumes. Their bodies were left in the pit until it was safe to recover them.

During that time, miners claimed to see the dead men carrying picks and shovels through the mountain snow. Their spirits didn't leave footprints or respond to any calls. When their bodies were finally recovered nearly a year later, it was discovered that a handful of the men had survived for a while in the shaft. They had built a raft in the rising water but died soon after, when the fire burned all the oxygen out of the shaft. Their bodies were buried and the hauntings ceased ... for a while.

On a night four years later, Dr. Clifford J. Owens entered the tunnel with James R. McKinstrey, a drilling operations superintendent. They had traveled for miles

Entrance to the Hoosac Tunnel.

into the dank tunnel when they stopped to rest. As Dr. Owens later wrote in a Michigan newspaper, "James and I stood there talking for a minute or two and were just about to turn back when suddenly I heard a strange mournful sound. It was just as if someone or something was suffering great pain.

"The next thing I saw was a dim light coming along the tunnel from a westerly direction. At first, I believed it was probably a workman with a lantern. Yet, as the light grew closer, it took on a strange blue color and appeared to change shape almost into the form of a human being without a head. The light seemed to be floating along about a foot or two above the tunnel floor. In the next instant, it felt as if the temperature had suddenly dropped and a cold, icy chill ran up and down my spine. The headless form came so close that I could have reached out and touched it but I was too terrified to move.

"For what seemed like an eternity, McKinstrey and I just stood there gaping at the headless thing . . . The blue light remained motionless for a few seconds as if it were actually looking us over, then floated off toward the east end of the shaft and vanished into thin air." Strange sights like this one continued throughout construction.

On Thanksgiving Day, 1874, the tunnel's last sixteen feet of rock were finally blasted out of what is still the longest tunnel in the United States. On February 9, 1875, the first train passed through it, one of hundreds of thousands since its opening. Yet the ghosts were not frightened off by the train traffic.

In 1976, Joseph Impoco, a worker who has spent more than fifty years at the railroad, was interviewed about his encounters with ghosts in the tunnel. He recalled one day when he was assigned to chip ice from the tracks by himself. In the dark of the tunnel, he heard an eerie voice cry out, "Joe! Joe! Joe! Jump quick." "I jumped all right," he told a newspaper reporter. "I leaped just like a frog" as an express train flew by him, barely missing him. After the close brush, he looked around to find who had warned him. No one was there.

After a few other times when unseen voices saved his life, Impoco quit the railroad for a safer job. But he continued to visit the spirits in the tunnel every year to thank them, saying, "If I don't, I feel something terrible will happen to me."

Virginia's Big Bull Tunnel, thought to be built in the early 1880s, has a long history of trouble, from rock slides to cave-ins to train crashes. In two different freak accidents in the tunnel, train engineers were thrown from their trains, crushing their skulls and killing them. During an inspection in 1905, it became clear that the tunnel was haunted. Inspectors heard moaning deep within the empty darkness. When one man bravely asked what the ghost wanted, it replied, "Remove that awful weight from my body . . . They are drinking my blood."

10

CHOOSING BLACK DEATH

The small village of Eyam in Derbyshire, England, commemorates "Plague Sunday" each year. During the last Sunday of August, the townspeople honor their ancestors who bravely endured an outbreak of the bubonic plague in 1665. Over the space of a year, this deadly disease killed more than 260 of the town's nearly 700 people.

That awful year saw many outbreaks of the deadly disease, known as the Black Death, which was spread by the bites of fleas found on rats. London was thought to have lost as many as 100,000 people to the plague, who died vomiting blood while their skin turned black.

What made the Eyam outbreak unusual was the choice the townspeople made when people began dying. Rather

The plague in London in 1665.

than risk spreading the disease to nearby villages, they made a pact that no one would leave or enter the town until people had stopped dying from the plague. This was amazingly heroic, as it meant there was no escape from a disease that for many meant certain death.

Today, a row of small houses in Eyam, called the "Plague Cottages," have signs on each home listing the residents who died there during 1665. It is one of the many places in this tragic town where ghosts of the dead are often felt or seen. Many see a sweet lady in a blue dress there who is said to wake people in the middle of the night.

☠ ☠ ☠

The Black Death came to Eyam in the form of fleas. They hitchhiked in on a bolt of damp cloth that came from disease-ridden London. George Viccars, a tailor's assistant who was in town to make clothes for a festival, unrolled the cloth before a fire to dry it out.

That's when the fleas carrying the plague escaped. Soon after, George became the plague's first victim, dying in agony on September 7, 1665. The disease spread quickly, killing more than forty villagers over the next few months.

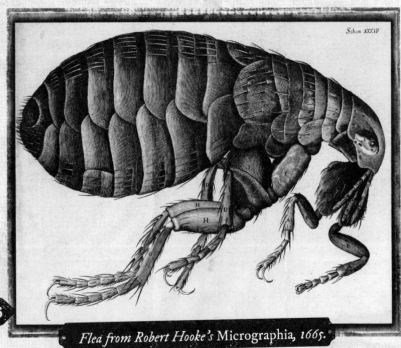

Flea from Robert Hooke's Micrographia, *1665.*

The cottage in Eyam where the plague began.

People were terrified. They didn't know how the disease spread and why some died and others didn't. When would they catch it and die? By spring, many talked of moving somewhere safer. But that would mean possibly bringing the plague with them.

The town's rector, William Mompesson, had just recently begun working at Eyam's church. He understood why people in his congregation were afraid. He was afraid too. William had sent his children away to relatives and begged his wife, Catherine, to leave as well, but she refused to leave his side. As the disease spread through the

William Mompesson.

town, he realized the same thing would happen in surrounding towns if people from Eyam fled there.

In June 1666, he joined forces with the former rector, Thomas Stanley, to see if the disease could somehow be stopped. He called an outdoor meeting in a field known as Cucklet Delf. There they asked the townspeople if they could be willing to stay in Eyam until the disease was no longer killing people, so it would not be spread to another town. Surprisingly, the townspeople agreed.

The town was cut off, or quarantined, from the outside world. Supplies from surrounding towns were left outside the village near a well. Money for the supplies was left in the hollows of a rock that were filled with vinegar, which was thought to kill the germs.

In an effort to stop the spread within the town, villagers were asked to stay home and the church was closed. It didn't stop the plague. Months passed, but villagers kept dying.

A doctor from 1720 described what it was like to die from the Black Death, which included:

—Nonstop vomiting, queasiness, and an inability to eat food

—Blood pouring from the nostrils, mouth, and butt

—Black, livid, bluish spots or blisters that burst underneath the skin

By August 1666, the weather was terribly hot, which made the fleas more active. As many as five people died each day in the small village. When entire families were wiped out, Marshall Howe, who had been infected and survived, often buried the dead. While he was immune, his family was not. One day he accidentally brought the plague back to his home, causing the death of his wife and young son.

When no one was available to help, people had to bury their own dead. One poor woman, Elizabeth Hancock, had six children and her husband die in the space of eight days. She buried them all herself at the family farm.

Even with death spreading all around them, no one in Eyam broke the quarantine. Pastor William Mompesson,

helped by his wife, Catherine, tried to ease the towns-people's suffering. But in letters sent to family, he wrote of the smell of "sadness and death" in the air. On August 22, Catherine caught the disease and died three days later.

In September and October, fewer people died. The disease was finally slowing down. On November 1, the farmworker Abraham Morten was the last of the 260 people in the village who would die of the plague. The people of Eyam had made the ultimate sacrifice, probably saving hundreds of lives.

On Plague Sunday, the story of the townspeople's her-oism is retold and a wreath is laid on the grave of Catherine Mompesson. But while the disease is long gone, some of its victims remain in the form of ghosts.

The Miners Arms pub, which was called the Kings Head when it was built in 1630, is said to be home to a few trapped souls, including an old woman in a black dress. Guests have heard footsteps and other strange occurrences so frightening, some have refused to stay the night.

In June 2016, a rider on the London Underground near Knightsbridge took a photo of what appears to be a ghost near the tracks. Paranormal investigators believe it was the spirit of a plague victim from the seventeenth century. The spirit was spotted near an ancient plague burial pit, which contains as many as one thousand victims of the Black Death outbreak of 1664.

SOME FINAL THOUGHTS

Seeing a ghost is frightening, especially after a terrible disaster. How would you react? Maybe instead of screaming and running, you could ask yourself, "Why am I afraid?"

Sure, the idea of dead people coming back to Earth is scary. But have you ever heard of a ghost actually hurting anyone? Ghost hunters have investigated thousands of sightings, but it's rare that anyone has been injured beyond maybe stumbling in the dark.

A ghost is usually more surprising than dangerous (unlike a poltergeist, which is an entirely different matter). The terror we feel when we encounter ghosts or ghost stories may be more about encountering the unknown, as well as a fear of death itself. Actual ghosts are often poor spirits stuck on Earth, forced to replay their death or an important part of their life over and over. They don't mean any harm; they just haven't accepted that they are dead.

I've never seen a ghost myself. But the more I learn, the more I want to meet one. When else will you get that close to a world beyond our own? So, happy hauntings!

FURTHER READING

1. "Have I Died?": 2011 Earthquake and Tsunami, Japan
Tarshis, Lauren. *I Survived the Japanese Tsunami, 2011*. Scholastic Inc., 2013.

2. No Way Out: 1911 Triangle Shirtwaist Fire, New York
Doman, Mary Kate. *Tragedy at the Triangle*. Arcadia Publishing, 2015.

3. White Death: 1910 Wellington Avalanche, Washington
Cuyle, Deborah. *The 1910 Wellington Disaster*. Arcadia Publishing, 2019.

4. Tornado Alley: 1908 Albertville Tornado, Alabama
Tarshis, Lauren. *Tornado Terror*. Scholastic Inc., 2017.

5. Iroquois Inferno: 1903 Iroquois Theater Fire, Illinois
Murphy, Jim. *The Great Fire*. Scholastic, Inc., 2006.

6. A Headless Haunting: 1900 Scofield Mine, Utah
Bartoletti, Susan Campbell. *Growing Up in Coal Country*. HMH Books for Young Readers, 1999.

7. The Little Ghosts of Galveston: 1900 Galveston Flood, Texas
Rogers, Lisa Waller. *The Great Storm*. Texas Tech University Press, 2010.

8. Ghost Train No. 9: 1891 Bostian Bridge Train Wreck, North Carolina
Reed, Robert C. *Train Wrecks*. Schiffer Publishing, 1997.

9. The Bloody Pit: 1860 Hoosac Tunnel, Massachusetts
Schexnayder, Cliff. *Builders of the Hoosac Tunnel*. Peter E. Randall Publisher, 2015.

10. Choosing Black Death: 1665 Eyam Plague, England
Barnard, Bryn. *Outbreak! Plagues that Changed History*. Dragonfly Books, 2015.

ACKNOWLEDGMENTS

I have to start by thanking my husband, Patrick, and daughters, Claire and Lila, who patiently listened to months of gruesome descriptions of disasters over dinner, and my sister, Heather, and nephew, Gray, who actually enjoy gore and ghosts and gave me great feedback. *Deadly Disasters* wouldn't have been published without my stalwart agent, Cathy Hemming, who kept assuring me that it was all just a matter of time. And finally, a huge thanks to everyone at Scholastic, especially the amazing Amanda Shih, who made my book so much better.

ABOUT THE AUTHOR

Photo courtesy of Judy Dunn

Dinah Williams is an editor and children's book author who is fascinated by odd and unusual stories. Her nonfiction books for children include *Terrible but True: Awful Events in American History*; *Secrets of Walt Disney World: Weird and Wonderful Facts About the Most Magical Place on Earth*; *Abandoned Amusement Parks*; and *Spooky Cemeteries*, which won the 2009 Children's Choice Award. She lives in beautiful Cranford, New Jersey, with her husband, two daughters, and two cats, none of whom enjoy a scary story.

KEEP READING FOR A
SPOOKY SNEAK PEEK AT
THE NEXT BOOK IN THE
TRUE HAUNTINGS SERIES
BY DINAH WILLIAMS:
BATTLEFIELD GHOSTS!

GHOSTS OF THE WESTERN FRONT

BATTLE OF VIMY RIDGE, FRANCE, APRIL 12, 1917

Much of World War I was fought in the trenches of the Western Front, a 400-mile stretch of battlefields through France to the coast of Belguim. The Allied and Central Power armies dug these long, deep ditches and then fought from the relative safety of underground. Occasionally an army would surge into the open space between the trenches, known as "No Man's Land." More often than not, that surge would get them killed. It was dangerous to recover the dead, so the bodies would often be left lying there.

Millions of soldiers lived for years in the trenches, which filled with mud when it rained and froze to ice when it was cold. Overrun with rats, lice, and fleas, the soldiers were never clean or dry and it was hard to sleep. Artillery would explode nearby, burying soldiers alive in the pits. So many bodies mixed in the bombed earth that hands, heads, and feet would poke out of the ground.

"We are all used to dead bodies or pieces of men, so much so that we are not troubled by the sight of them," wrote one Canadian soldier. "There was a right hand sticking out of the trench in the position of a man trying to shake hands with you, and as the men filed out they would often grip it and say, 'So long, old top, we'll be back again soon.'"

Frank Iriam, a sniper in the 1st Canadian Division, described how frightening it was to be alongside these fallen soldiers on the Western Front. "You could feel the pulse of the thousands of dead with their pale hands protruding through the mud here and there and seeming to beckon you," he wrote in his memoir. "You could feel the presence of something not of this earth. Akin to goblins." And Frank was not the only soldier haunted by their spirits.

Another Canadian soldier wrote to his mother that, "One night while carrying bombs, I had occasion to take cover when about twenty yards off I saw you looking towards me as plain as life." Shocked, he crawled toward this vision of his mother. A German shell suddenly exploded where he had previously been. "Had it not been for you, I certainly would have been reported 'missing,'" the soldier wrote. "You'll turn up again, won't you, mother, next time a shell is coming?"